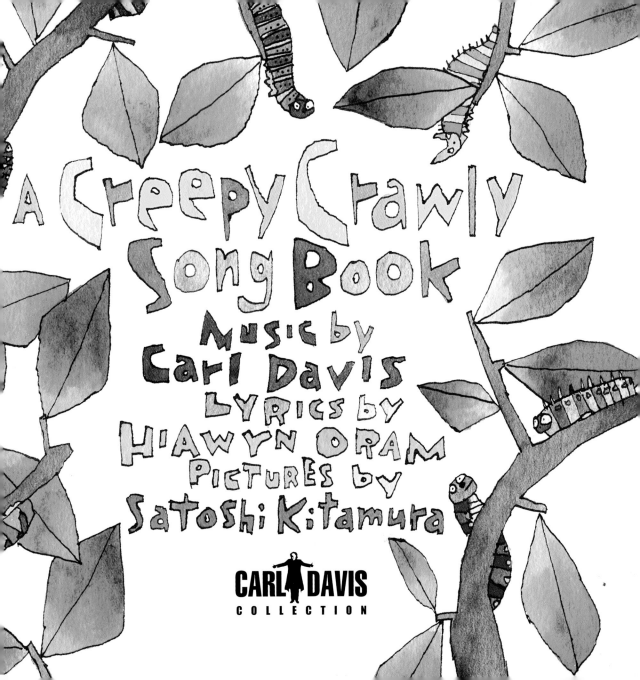

A Creepy Crawly Song Book

Music by Carl Davis
Lyrics by Hiawyn Oram
Pictures by Satoshi Kitamura

CARL DAVIS COLLECTION

"Insects share many characteristics of humans: they live to eat, procreate and die. It is the variety of ways they play this out that attracted me to Hiawyn Oram's delightful and sometimes challenging cycle of poems. Her insects polka, march, waltz and sing the Blues. I loved setting them. And I hope you enjoy reading, playing and singing them as well as being amazed by Satashi's beautiful illustrations."

From Carl and the Carl Davis Collection

A Creepy Crawly Song Book

CONTENTS

1. A HUNDRED FEET AHEAD

I've a centipedal body
I've a hundred feet in all
I can move about like lightning
I don't have to creep or crawl
I can dash about the greenhouse
I can dart without a thought
I'm so quick to seize my quarry
It don't know that it's been caught.

And when it comes to footwork
With the kind of legs I've got
You should really see my Cancan
And my Rumba and Gavotte.

(DANCE OF THE CENTIPEDE)

For… I've… this… centipedal body
It's the way that I've been bred
And no matter what I'm doing
I'm a hundred feet ahead.
I can rush around the garden
I can burrow through the ground
I can get away from danger
Fast as danger comes around.

And when it comes to footwork
With the kind of legs I've got
You should really see my Charleston
And my Centipedal Trot.

Slow, slow snail
Slow, slow snail
Taking forever to
    cross a leaf
If you don't hurry up
    you will come to grief
Slow, slow snail.

Slow, slow snail
Slow, slow snail
Whatever you do, don't cross that path
There's a plump young thrush in the stone birdbath
With a beady eye on your shining trail
Slow, slow snail.

Slow, slow snail
Slow, slow snail
You took forever to cross that leaf
You couldn't make haste and you came to grief
In the beak of a common or garden thief
Now all that's left is your shining trail
But no slow snail
No slow snail
No… slow… snail…

Itchy Scritchy

Itchy scritchy, scratch my head
The Lice have put their kids to bed
In my crown of golden hair
Itchy scritchy, it's not fair.

Susie's hair is nicer
Emma's hair is longer
Jason's hair is thicker
Andy's hair is stronger
Mary's hair is dirty
Dan's sits up and begs
So why's it always MY hair
Where they lay their eggs?

Itchy scritchy, scratch my head
The Lice have put their kids to bed
Itchy scritchy, scratch and shout
HOW'LL I EVER GET THEM OUT!

Walking Sticks

4.

Still as the night
When the wind drops
Still as a kite
When the breeze stops
Still as the grave, silent and cold
Still as a tale that's never been told
Till the sun sets
And the night falls
Till the light ends
And the dark calls
Is it the wind?
Eyes playing tricks?
This tree is alive
With Walking Sticks!

CONFESSION OF A PRAYING MANTIS

Oh, they think I'm very pious
And they think I'm very good
'Cause it looks as though I'm praying
Like a holy Brahman would
And it looks as though I'm patient
Otherworldly, on my knees
Begging favours of our Maker
Saying thank you, saying please.

But the truth is I'm not praying
I'm not rev'rent, I'm no saint
That is only the impression
And the picture that I paint
No, the truth is I'm not godly
I'm ungrateful, and I'm rude
And the only words of prayer I know
Are GIMME, GIMME FOOD.

b. March of the

Left right left, left right left
The Soldier Ants are here to say
We'll guard the nest as best we may
For the Queen is laying her eggs today
Left right left, left right left.

The Nursemaid Ants are standing by
To wash and feed the young larvae
The Cleaner Ants have cleared the ground
Of scraps and husks left lying around
For the Queen is laying her eggs today
Left right left, left right left.

The Miller Ants have ground the wheat
Until it's fine enough to eat
The Farmer Ants have milked the herd
Of fat young aphids: pass the word
For the Queen is laying her eggs today
Left right left, left right left.

WorkerAnts

The Barrel Ants are filled to burst
With honeydew in case of thirst
The Gardener Ants have grown a crop
Of fine fresh fungus and can't stop
For the Queen is laying her eggs today
Left right left, left right left.

The Soldier Ants will guard the nest
The Nursemaid Ants will do their best
The Cleaner Ants have cleared the ground
The Miller Ants the wheat have ground
The Farmer Ants have milked the herd
The Barrel Ants are full, my word
The Gardener Ants have grown a feast
While the Hunter Ants have bagged a beast
For the Queen has LAID her eggs today
Hurray, hurray, hurray!
Hurray, hurray, hurray!

7. CAN OF WORMS

A can of wriggling, wiggling worms
Stood by a babbling brook
The talk was all of who'd be next
Upon the fisherman's hook.
"Not me," said the Pink, "I'm far too thin."
"Not me," said the Grey, "I won't give in."
"Not me," said the Brown, "it's not my line."
"Then you," said the fisherman, "you'll do fine."

A can of wriggling, wiggling worms
Stood by that babbling brook
The talk was all of how to get
From off a fisherman's hook.
"You jump," said the Pink, "you can't go wrong."
"You wind," said the Grey, "but don't take long."
"You swim," said the Brown, "or else you float."
That's right," said the fisherman, "down a throat."

An empty can without a worm
Stood by that babbling brook
The talk was none, they all had gone
To bait the fisherman's hook.
"I jumped," said the Pink, "into a trout."
"I wound," said the Grey, "now let me out."
"I swam," said the Brown, "but far too late."
"That's right," said the fisherman, "you did great!"

FLEA CIRCUS

Cat Fleas, Rat fleas, Hedgehog and Bird
The circus is a comin' or haven't you heard?
Every kind of flea, even kitten and pup
The circus is a comin', roll up, roll up!

There'll be bareback riders, there'll be acrobats
There'll be feats of strength, there'll be daring acts
There'll be flying through the air with the greatest of ease
There'll be Madam Chow from China and her Dancing Fleas.

Cat fleas, Fat fleas, Hamster and Mouse
And every kind of flea from hedgerow and house
Come and take your seat, get your full moment's worth
At the Great Flea Circus that's the Smallest Show on Earth!

9. Battle of the Stags

There was no growl, there was no snarl
There was no warning sound
As Beetle One, that Mighty Stag
Prepared to stand his ground
For Beetle Two, so young and keen
Would make the branch his own
And raised his horns to give the sign
He'd fight this out alone.

The Mighty Stag, the young Greenhorn
Now locked in deadly wrest
And who could see the other off
Would be the final test
So up and down that slender branch
Those battling Beetles went
Their armour held and gave no sign
Of chip or chink or dent.

And then at last the Mighty Stag
A winning grasp had found
And lifting up the young Greenhorn
He threw him to the ground
The Greenhorn lay defeated there
But still one punch would pack
And raised his head and loudly hissed
"O.K. – BUT I'LL BE BACK!"

10. BUSYBEE

The businessman is busy, he is busy being busy
The doctor is so busy that she sometimes drops
The porter on the platform, he is very, very busy
The mother of four children never stops
But of all the very busy things that you or I will see
The busiest of all of them must be the busy bee.

(Chorus)
Busy in the bushes and busy in the field
Sipping all the nectar that each flower can yield
Busy in the beehive and busy in the trees
Busy feeding future busy, busy, busy bees.

The hornet is so busy, it just buzzes it's so busy
The firefly is a-busy giving off a glow
The butterfly is flat out going flitter flutter flat out
The slug is kept quite busy going slow
But of all the very busy things that you or I will see
The busiest of all of them must be the busy bee.

(Repeat chorus)

The businessman is busy, he is busy being busy
The housewife is so busy that she sometimes weeps
The waitress in the diner, she is very, very busy
The watchman who's on duty never sleeps
But of all the very busy things that you or I will see
The busiest of all of them must be the busy bee.

(Repeat chorus)

Busy, busy, busy, busy, busy, busy, busy…

11. Living A Day
(SONG OF THE MAYFLY)

Born in the morning
Married at noon
Buried at sunset
Death, you're too soon.
Living a lifetime
All in a day
Living a lifetime
For one day in May.

Born for the moment
Caught in the dance
Come, let us take it
While there's a chance.
Living a lifetime
All in a day
Living a lifetime
For one day in May.

Born to be mayflies
Born not to last
Seizing the present
As it flies past.
Living a lifetime
All in a day
Living a liftime
For one day in May.

The Black Widow's Waltz

Black widow's grieving
Her husbands keep leaving
Her children and her on their own.
She's fiercely berating
Such cowardly mating
That leaves a poor widow alone.

Black Widow's wailing
And Black Widow's railing
And Black Widow's dead against men.
She's pursing and pouting
And def'nitely doubting
She'll ever get married again.

Black widow's crying
Her husbands keep dying
As soon as each wedding is done.
She's loudly complaining
There're no men remaining
Forgetting she ATE EVERY ONE!

13. A CREEPY CRAWLY CATERPILLAR

A creepy crawly caterpillar
Lay upon a leaf
His body full of milkweed sap
His thoughts weighed down with grief.
"I do not have a feathered plume
Nor yet a velvet wing
I cannot flit, I cannot fly
I am an ugly thing
And yet I'm sure that deep inside
A-struggling to be free
There is some other character
There is another me."

Then creepy crawly caterpillar
Made himself a bed
And tucked up tight and fell asleep
And dreamed his dreams instead.
"I do so want a feathered plume
And, more, a velvet wing
I long to flit, I long to fly
To be a lovely thing
I am so sure that deep inside
A-struggling to be free
There is some other character
There is another me."

And as it was, that caterpillar
From his sleep did wake
And took a breath and stretched a leg
And gave himself a shake.
"I seem to have a feathered plume
A velvet painted wing
I seem to flit, I seem to fly
I am a lovely thing
I was so sure deep down inside
A-struggling to be free
There was some other character ...
A butterfly – that's me!"

14.

Uurgh, Eegh, Ugh

Uurgh, eegh, ugh
A green and slimy slug
Have you ever met such a wobbily blob
Such a slippery, slithery sluggardly slob
But another slug?
Another slug!

Uurgh, eegh, ugh,
A green and slimy slug,
Who could ever love such a wobbily blob
Such a livery, slivery, sluggardly slob
But another slug?
Another slug!

15. Mama Mosquito's Midnight Whine

The midnight hour is creepin'
Baby lies a-sleepin'
Underneath her veil of net so fine
She stirs and wakes to hear it
And she doesn't know to fear it
Mama Mosquito's Midnight Whine.

"A little bitty meal
A little drink of blood
Is all I ask of you
Baby, sweet rosebud
A little fragrant nip
Can that be such a sin?
Now open up your net
Baby, please let me in."

The midnight dew is glist'nin'
Baby is a-list'nin'
Underneath her veil of net so fine
She smiles where she is layin'
At the band she thinks is playin'
Mama Mosquito's Whine.

"A little bitty meal
A little drink of blood
Is all I ask of you
Baby, sweet rosebud
A little bitty sip
Can that do any harm?
My laying time is near
Baby, throw out an arm."

The gate of dawn unlatches
Baby frets and scratches
Underneath her veil of net so fine
She cries where she is layin'
Bitten hard by all that playin'
Of Mama Mosquito's Midnight Whine …
Mama Mosquito's …
Midnight …
Whine …

LAMENT OF THE HOUSE FLY

16.

Oh, to be a Robber Fly, some other fly but me
A Crane Fly or a Fruit Fly or a Brother Fly, not me.
The House Fly is so hated
It's so hounded , underrated
That I'd rather be most any fly but me.

I'd rather be a Caddis Fly, a Dung Fly, or a Drone
I'd even be a Tsetse, working jungles on my own.
The House Fly's life is fated
From the start incriminated
Oh, I'd rather be most any fly but me.

I'd rather be a Flower Fly, a Stalk-Eye, or a Bee
I'd love to be a Horse Fly in a hunting stablery.
The House Fly's Fate's allotted –
There you see, I've just been swatted
And a Dead Fly, very Dead Fly
NOW THAT'S ME.

17. Ladybird's Lullaby

Hush, little lovebugs, don't say a word
The moon's in the sky and the nightjar is heard
The glow worms are glowing, the fireflies peep,
And you, my little lovebugs, must now go to sleep.

Hush, little darlings, don't make a sound
The stars are a-lit and the dew's on the ground
The bat wings are whirring, the owl is awake,
And you should be in bed, yes, **now for heaven's sake!**

Hush, little lovebugs, don't say a word
The moon's in the sky and the nightjar is heard
The glowworms are glowing, the fireflies peep,
And you, my little lovebugs, are now… fast… aslee… eep…

Carl Davis (CBE) was born in New York in 1936 and came to the UK in 1960. Davis is a true music-maker and all-round musician, as both conductor and composer. He has changed the face of concerts as we know them, making classical music both accessible and varied and is a consummate showman and a first rate entertainer. His career has spanned many genres, from silent film performances to his popular themed concerts such as *An Evening with James Bond* and *Oscar Winners*. He is perhaps most well known for his music for television including the series *The World At War*, BBC's *Pride & Prejudice* and *Cranford*, ITV's *Goodnight Mr. Tom*, and the award winning film, *The French Lieutenant's Woman*.

Hiawyn Oram grew up in South Africa. As a child she had a wooden Wendy House which she shared with the local insect population. She's been at home with creepy crawlies ever since. After graduating from the University of Kwa Zulu Natal in English and Drama, she worked as an advertising copywriter before becoming a full-time writer. She's written many children's books published in many languages across the world, including Chinese, Russian, Korean, Taiwanese, Japanese, Polish, Greek, Basque and Catalan and won several awards. She also writes poetry and book and lyrics for musicals. Dreamworks (DWA) have optioned her last series starring a reluctant witch's familiar, as the inspiration for an upcoming animated movie entitled *Rumblewick*.

Satoshi Kitamura was born in Japan in 1956. He lived in the UK from the early 1980's until 2009 working as a picture book illustrator and author. He illustrated several of Hiawyn Oram's earliest books, such as *Angry Arthur*, which won the Mother Goose Award for Illustration, *In The Attic* and *Ned & The Joybaloo* all still in print today. He has written and illustrated many texts of his own including *The Comic Adventure Of Boots, When Sleep Cannot Sleep, Igor, The Bird Who Cannot Sing* and *Millie's Marvellous Hat*. He now lives in Japan.

Soloist: Sarah Eyden

Children's Choir: Eton Wick C of E First School

Piano: Catherine Edwards, Carl Davis (CBE)

Percussion: Stephen Henderson, Gary Kettle

Produced & Engineered by: Steve Parr

Executive Producer: Jessie Stevenson

Label Manager: Charles Padley

Graphic Design: N9Design.com

With special thanks to: Andrew Eggleton, Mr. R Harris, Lucie Cook, Jean Boht, Annette Borrett, Penny Hopwood, Graham Warren, Victoria McCalla,

Recorded at Eton Wick C of E First School and Air Edel, 2011